D0699210

ALSO BY MARY JO SALTER

POEMS

The Surveyors (2017)

Nothing by Design (2013)

A Phone Call to the Future:
New and Selected Poems (2008)

Open Shutters (2003)

A Kiss in Space (1999)

Sunday Skaters (1994)

Unfinished Painting (1989)

Henry Purcell in Japan (1985)

FOR CHILDREN

The Moon Comes Home (1989)

ZOOM ROOMS

ZOOM ROOMS

POEMS

MARY JO SALTER

ALFRED A. KNOPF   NEW YORK   2022

THIS IS A BORZOI BOOK
PUBLISHED BY ALFRED A. KNOPF

Copyright © 2022 by Mary Jo Salter

All rights reserved.
Published in the United States by Alfred A. Knopf,
a division of Penguin Random House LLC, New York,
and distributed in Canada by Penguin Random House
of Canada Limited, Toronto.

www.aaknopf.com

Knopf, Borzoi Books, and the colophon are
registered trademarks of Random House LLC.

Library of Congress Cataloging-in-Publication Data
Names: Salter, Mary Jo, author.
Title: Zoom rooms : poems / Mary Jo Salter.
Description: New York : Alfred A. Knopf, 2022.
Identifiers: LCCN 2021038888 (print) | LCCN 2021038889 (ebook) |
ISBN 9780593321317 (hardcover) | ISBN 9780593321324 (ebook)
Subjects: LCGFT: Poetry.
Classification: LCC PS3569.A46224 Z66 2022 (print) |
LCC PS3569.A46224 (ebook) | DDC 811/.54—dc23
LC record available at https://lccn.loc.gov/2021038888
LC ebook record available at https://lccn.loc.gov/2021038889

Jacket art and design by Chip Kidd

Manufactured in Canada
First Edition

for Kathleen Lormina Cowart
("Leena")

CONTENTS

PART ONE

YOUR SESSION HAS TIMED OUT

due to inactivity.
Do you want to reboot
back to your nativity?

Too bad. You can't go back.
Or forward, for that matter.
Remember running track,

dunking a basketball,
or, come to think of it, doing
anything at all?

Too bad. You can't reboot.
In fact, the very terms
you use will soon be moot,

will take their downward spiral
like you to a black hole
while brave new words go viral—

assuming being "active"
or "inactive" is a thing
in the future. Or to "live."

ORECCHIETTE

The trattoria crowd
is so loud we keep leaning
forward to be heard.

Again: "What did you say?"
he asks, cupping an ear.
"I'm having the *orecchiette*,"

I tell him—tripping there
the obedient neurons tracking
back to Apulia, where

my mother and I, hosted
by distant, just-met cousins,
were led to a wide bed

sprinkled with flower petals.
"In fact it wasn't flowers"—
I'm warming to my tale—

"but pasta, ear-shaped, eggy,
handmade *orecchiette*
spread on the beds to dry.

Get it? Ear is *orecchio*.
Like the French for ear, *oreille*.
And like *oreiller*, pillow."

Heaps of translated ears
sleeping at noon, then wakened
to feed me all these years

later—why be beholden
(given all I've forgotten)
to this little scene?

Italianness, for starters—
a pride in being related
to a place, like a first course—

but things that happened after
have been poured on like a sauce
and given it a stir.

All the delicious days
I've eaten, unrecorded,
all the poems and plays

on words I was too lazy
to set down, and are gone!
Nor am I yet ready

to tell even the patient
man who shares my pillow
why I've fallen silent.

"Looks really good," I shout
at his lasagna while
thinking *I should find out*

which cousins are still alive . . .
It occurs to me: I am.
Do I catch a whiff

of courage off my plate
of *orecchiette?* A little
taste of what I should write?

CARLO CRIVELLI AND THE TREES

Playful, prolific, noted for
tableaux of bounty, he'd do a portrait
of a man's face composed of fruit,
or picture his Madonnas under

garlands, bright as chandeliers,
of nearly three-D pickles, pears,
apples pecked by birds; then turn
even a gruesome Crucifixion

into a sort of game. Here: a
trompe-l'oeil in oil and tempera
replicates the look of wood on
a panel that is truly wooden,

in fact paints over knots to make
knots in the hard planes of the cross.
Real as a relic, the unique
tree on which one man-god dies

while mourners on both sides gaze up,
their tresses patterned like wood grain
again, the dry eyes in their deep-
lined faces weeping beads of sap,

and in that surfacing of sorrow
each arrested teardrop tough
as an acorn, as if there to sow
millennia of grief.

What excuse then for the lustrous
finish on the instrument
of torture set before that sparse
landscape? What could be meant

by the assorted grayish, spindly
background saplings, barely a leaf
(though it is spring) alive?
Should we write off existence simply

as a pale prequel to the tale
of afterlife? False question for
him, probably, inclined to honor
foremost his material,

which is to say the fresh-cut trees
splintered into delicate
paintbrushes, or hewn as flat
massive planks to soak up these

minerals and plants ground down
to the consistency of paints
that may, or may not, blossom in
the ways the maker wants.

WHITE PETALS, 3 A.M.

Lights out but it's glowing—
the dogwood's white-petaled cloud that fills
the window above the window seat
just feet from the foot of my bed.

And I'm thinking I've seen this,
the same wide-eyed whiteness, winter nights
when the naked branches were gloved in snow
that had stored the day's light somehow.

Now it's the moon
(an assumed one, out of the window's frame)
spilling light on the constellations
of blossoms, beamed through the room

to interrogate me: should people sleep
in April? The flowering out there
could be my lit-up circuitry,
my brain reflecting

on bounty. This. The moon of conscious
fullness. The brimming thing that wanes.
The tree with every fragile
petal on before the first

one falls, the sun comes up, the green
leaves take over the length of summer,
so long you forget you live in time.
Don't blink. Don't. Not again.

OAK HILL, WEST VIRGINIA

C. Robert Cooke, 1929–2017

"Great louts are necessary
at funerals," Julian Barnes
wrote in *Flaubert's Parrot,*
a book I had just read—
in fact, it was in the car
I'd parked at the cemetery—

and so I thought of that,
some witty argument
to shore up against grief.
My friend had lost her father,
and although he wasn't mine
to mourn for, I'd revered him.

I stood there as his grown
children traded jokes
about their Gregory Peck
look-alike, coal-country
barber's son who'd risen
to glory as a doctor.

Remember how Mom said
(they said again) that Dad
had been elected second-
handsomest man in college?
(A pause, for full effect.)
Who was the *other* guy?

At last came two great louts,
two bruisers in T-shirts
(one of which read PROUD
TO BE AN AMERICAN)
hired to sink the weight
of the old man's coffin

into his native soil.
No, a small box of ashes.
They lowered it and then,
respectfully, their heads.
Why, really, were they here,
or the last-minute preacher?

A skinny boy aswim
in a man's threadbare suit
and just a little lame,
he walked up with his cane
like a bishop's scepter.
Everything off-kilter,

beginning with the hint
of atheists among
the party that had hired him,
and then there was that key ring,
gigantic, dangling from
the belt that barely held

his baggy trousers up.
At last his volume too
went up. His voice was clear.
It's been a year . . . I've kept
wanting to say something,
anything, so true.

He said he saw his father
in his own shaving mirror.
Just that; made the claim
our images don't vanish
wholly, or at once.
And when he had to end

by calling on Our Father
in his Kingdom, I even thought
(not laughing, not entirely)
He's got Saint Peter's keys.
Then we all shook his hand
and the hands of both the louts.

I walked back to my car,
lump in my throat, not quite
ready to make peace
with what I was; and prayed
for the hidden, vivid face
that smiled at me in childhood.

THE FORTUNE COOKIE

No one remembers anymore
what the fortune cookie said.
What's come down in family lore
is that it was *read:*

that is, that it was she
who read it, though she was only three.
The two nice daycare ladies
had stood by as she flipped

open the Sleeping
Beauty lunch box;
observed her as she slipped
the cubes of cheese, the apple slices

into the obedient mouth
that had been promised
the cookie as reward.
Then she cracked it as you would

a new-laid egg,
and out spilled the golden
present of a long long sentence
and all their cries of praise.

Her father came in his car.
Yes, it was he who'd taught her
the game, letter by letter.
We tested her, they told him,

with other words, and everyone
who'd doubted her was wrong!
What would she be when she grew up?
Some masterpiece of a thing.

She wasn't listening.
The future was a sweet
to eat tomorrow, with a secret
on the tip of its paper tongue.

MAN-BARBIES

That's how my two daughters
referred to their two Kens—
just two of them, among the legions
of leggy, big-haired Barbies,
each of whom went to bed alone
and had plenty of room
in her own sedan-shaped
box of Kleenex.
One by one, not meaning to skew
the ultimate balance of the sexes,
I'd bought girl-dolls
for birthdays and Christmases,
or because it was nobody's
birthday or holiday
but my girls wanted something new.

Me too. I tired of hacked-off hairdos
after the games of Beauty Parlor;
of tiny high heels without a mate;
of permanently tiptoed feet
smeared in nail polish
like bloody excuses for shoes.
Yet rarely did buying a fresh Ken
seem any kind of solution.
And since Man-Barbies
didn't even care what they wore,

why get them extra clothes?
Besides, my girls
were clearly growing too old for dolls.
I was shocked one day to overhear
a Barbie had had an abortion.

Which Ken had been the father?
Or was that even a question?
Man-Barbies were an enigma.
Maybe each Ken was a token
husband for my girls themselves,
in which case
there mustn't be more.
Could it be that one Man-Barbie stood
for their dad, and the other
for the brother they'd never had?

Too much interpretation, surely.
My daughters liked girl-Barbies,
being girly. Which meant they chose
one day to sashay out as women
in their own Barbie heels
and looked around amazed, as I had once:
how many Man-Barbies
were out there, each of them
wanting something new!

SILK BLOUSE

An old, pilled, faded blouse
I'd nearly thrown away
a dozen times was what I wore that day.
Maybe I'd dreamed

that with some talisman
I could keep things the same?
But then the surgeon studied your report.
I drove us home,

neither of us said much,
I turned on the kettle, brought
us both some tea;
we sat stunned on the couch.

And then your tears.
My lovely girl, your tears.
The sobbing bravery
you showed in facing up

to what you felt,
head buried on my shoulder,
young tears soaking through
old blouse and older mother.

That night I threw the stained
thing in the trash; a second
thought and I fished it out.
It went back in my closet

unwashed, not to be worn
ever again, not even
on the day we know you're well,
which you will be:

I wanted its polka dots
to go on staring at me,
to say: *never, never,*
never forget how she suffered.

ST. SEBASTIAN INTERCEDING FOR THE PLAGUE-STRICKEN

Josse Lieferinxe, c. 1499

At the arch of the city gate,
two rolling wheels are caught
in one halted moment:
the back half of a horse
harnessed to the front
of a cart that serves as hearse
for a pile of swaddled corpses.

What crops their little scene
is more city, pressing in—
castellated turrets,
fortifications, courtyards,
churches with a recurrence
of steeples like arrowheads
stuck in the pint-sized saint

who prays but feels no pain:
loinclothed Sebastian
kneels on a tatty patch
of cirrus, while brown-bearded,
red-cloaked, hearty Jesus
on heaps of cumulus
lifts a hand in blessing.

White is for the one
robed angel billowing
below him like more clouds,
white is for the cassocks

on the tonsured monks
performing obsequies
over earthbound bodies,

white is for the shrouds
on the dead set down in streets
that once held milling crowds—
shrouds tight as bandages,
each one a chrysalis
that hoped to be undone,
awaken, fly in bliss

up to eternity,
although the sky contends
with the angel's opposite,
a beaked, bat-like, web-footed,
winged demon of some sort
who wields above its head
an object that's a cross

between cross and battle-ax.
Some sicken behind doors,
but one foregrounded man
(hired to slip another's
body into a body-
shaped, expectant hollow,
a grave like a man's shadow)

is pictured in the instant
he himself is stricken:
arms raised in agony
as a woman raises hers
in lament, his sleeves are green,
the only green, and large
as life, larger than any

thing which floating, tiny
Sebastian has time to say.

PART TWO

ZOOM ROOMS

Followers and Friends and Participants,
Gallery View, which Speaker View supplants,
Meeting Attendants, who for now are Mute
or worse, Unmute, a word I might dispute
even exists, whether verb or adjective:
Is this life? Is this how you want to live?
Nose-scratches broadcast, thoughts shrunk to an icon
or two (Clap, Thumbs Up), and if you leave your mic on
while others talk, your faintest sighing framed
in gold light like a vanity mirror? Named
on your little tile, you can't slip out unseen.
Self-surveilled, your eye contact on-screen
seems off. Don't look at people! Focus where
the tiny camera is that proves you're there.

*

Bookcase-prop and real or fake bouquet
behind you, well-dressed only to the waist
as if in a casket, top half on display,
here's another weirdness to be faced:
you're in the Gallery. You're shown as one
of your own satellites—as if the sun
were both a planet and the Copernican
magnet for all planets. Yes, I can
undo all this and activate the Hide
Self feature . . . where was that again? It's hidden
nearly as neatly as the moon's dark side.
But that's like suicide. It feels forbidden
now that I'm linked to the beloved spectator
who is myself: light-source and shadowed crater.

*

Here, as professor, I am Host; Enable
the Waiting Room, and one by one Admit
my students etherized around a table
in the Platonic classroom where they sit—
or recline in bed. Protest this? I don't dare.
Full roster: nobody's ill! Smile and wave
hello, a new habit. *Can you hear me?* Share
Screen, clicking a doc I thought to Save
to Desktop on my laptop. This is normal.
Mixed metaphors, and no term we have chosen
ourselves. Whether our verse was free or formal,
we thought we were free thinkers . . . *Oops, you're frozen,*
we're bound to say. We sign on for more jargon.
Paste in the password, try to Join again.

*

The baby has been brought up in a bubble.
No "outside people." She's Generation C
for coronavirus—naturally, somebody
clever came up already with that label
to spread like another germ. OK, Boomer
is what I am, and on a whim or weekends
her mother, my Millennial offspring, sends
an Invitation. Am I in the room or
am I not? To find out, Leena leans
forward to try to taste my virtual head
and failing at that, lifts a lightbulb-screwing
sort of wave, a wrist-twist like a queen's.
Real life at a social distance, almost dead,
what on earth can she think we think we're doing?

*

You're done, Randall. You were my first Zoomed
memorial service—sadly, not the last.
Was it recorded? Will it be exhumed
one day to show the mourners of the past—
the talking heads in rows who told old stories
about you, laughing, crying—unaware
we're under headstones in real cemeteries?
On the other hand: who says what's really there?
Memory zooms you back, a neuro-heaven.
I see you still, wiping a dripping brow
with your ever-ready giant handkerchief.
Shocking you died (of "something else"), and even
stranger you're more present in our grief:
more three-dimensional than we are now.

*

By the time these sonnets fit into a book,
blocks on a page, an old technology
happily unremarkable as the pre-
pandemic world, how odd will it look
that we're solid flesh again? Someday soon,
the few corporeal beings we dare see—
grocery clerks and nurses, EMT
drivers, the essential Amazon
delivery guys who ring the bell and run,
the letter carriers who bear their worry
as to what spiky cells homebodies carry—
will be everyone. Reader, you took the vaccine,
you threw away your masks, you're hugging, kissing.
As for your avatar—is that you, missing

*

your mirror-image mirage? Do you Schedule
more Meetings to screen, like movies? Do you tell
friends you could safely fly to see that travel
is, what with climate change, an ethical
problem after all? Think of the solitary
walks you used to take: though you were wary
of other walkers, and stepped into the street
unspeaking as they approached (an etiquette
of mandatory rudeness), have you found
yourself less patient now that there's more sound?
Loud diners. Children. And nowhere a Mute button.
So much else from the old days you'd forgotten
and might sacrifice, if that were possible . . .
people, basically?
               End Meeting for All.

PART THREE

MULE TEAM AND POSTER

Walker Evans's photograph; Donald Justice's poem

Words change the image. SILAS GREEN SHOW
is the strange phrase on the poster pasted
to the brick warehouse wall, which fills its space

with no wish to shape things, or to turn a corner
any more than sky has. And yet I read SILAS
as silo, I read GREEN as what turns to hay.

And with these words the dancing girls
on the poster promoting the long-ago
upcoming SHOW in their Flapper dresses

seem fringed with straw; seem to impose
their plane on the plane of the mule and cart
in front of the wall, the actual

weight of real women on his back—
as real as he, anyway, a three-
dimensional mule before Evans took

the picture. Only now do I discern
the mule as a team, that in fact the profile
of one mule's head is multiple—

dumb animal that I am, the double
between the mule and the wall escaped me
like an eye-blink frame in a movie.

And with that, the brick wall itself, not merely
the dancing girls, starts traveling left
on that cart that nonetheless is still

what Evans framed, and Justice, who
saw Alabama and sun after rain;
and what you, viewer of photographs

and reader of poems, made when you said
"how could people not see *that?*"—
the layers you alone brought to it.

VANITAS

Look: the sockets in the skull
set on the table with a jumble
of other stuff—a pocket watch,
a mug, a manuscript, a candle,
a crumpled, stiff cloth hanging off—

can't see that the artist's palette
(whose vivid, skull-sized counterfeit,
heavy with great gobs of color,
is painted into a corner) has
a thumbhole in it like a socket.

Everything's inanimate
except the wit. On a false ledge,
brushes currently in use
are laid down nonetheless; top right,
perfectly intact, the canvas

is rendered peeling from its frame,
and dangling there is a self-portrait—
a little oval like a locket
ladies of quality once wore.
You ask the artist's name?

I can't read my notes here. All
I have is this picture in my phone . . .
It's Flemish, and I think on loan
from a gallery in Hull.
Trust me, he's forgotten,

but isn't it wonderful, the skull-
palette with the black look of
an eye scooped out? I think I'd feel
great if I'd thought of that, at least
for a little while.

SCRABBLE

Because they both were angry, they fell silent.
Or not quite. Bob was the one who'd never meant
to say much in the first place. He was stable
emotionally, he didn't need to babble
on about feelings. Why wasn't she content
to let things go? And what a strange announcement
she'd made: "This time I won't speak till you're able
to ask what's wrong. I'm tired of prompting." Well,
he'd take that threat, or promise, as her full
permission not to ask her. So he bent
over his book, and lived in its word-bubble
perfectly successfully for a while
until Kay couldn't stand it. He knew she wouldn't.
She was surprised when Bob agreed to Scrabble.

Kay was the one who brought it to the table,
got a pencil, confirmed she'd have no trouble
tallying points; offered a compliment
for each word Bob set down. Oh, the ancient
peacemaking of women! Hard to tell
if men or women hate it more. So well
were these two suited, though, that with a skill
derived from practice, each sought their own double
and triple word scores as a means to hobble
the obstinate opponent; to prevent
basically anything, anywhere they went.
Shrugging, sighing, all their options spent,
they stopped mid-game. She said first, "I can't go,
can you?" "I have bad letters," he said. "No."

ITALIAN HAIKU

You spotted them first
at the Spanish Steps' florist:
bought me those tulips.

*

Vatican map room:
there's my grandparents' birthplace,
Castellaneta!

*

Domed by umbrellas,
we left the long line, bummed to
give up St. Peter's.

*

At the Uffizi,
we sliced minutes from timeless
paintings for pizza.

*

Are the Brownings in?
Let's go back to check, via
the Ponte Vecchio.

*

Yes, a strained ankle:
but give me more cobblestoned
hills in Siena.

*

The mausoleum
of Galla Placidia:
nothing has died here!

*

Airport hotel? No,
on our last night I want to
not have a last night.

*

Thanks, taxi driver—
when you got lost, we circled
the Colosseum.

JOHN SINGER SARGENT: TWO INTERIORS

The Breakfast Table, c. 1883–84

Violet and orange—
that's to say, his teenaged
sister Violet

trying to cut
through a piece of fruit
without looking at it:

she's absorbed in an open
book propped up on
more oranges,

and her appetite
for the next page, her
own luminous future

is reflected in glints
on the silver vase
of blush-pink roses,

in the streak of milky
light down the jug
of white porcelain,

not to mention
the blank space hanging
in the Japanese scroll

on the wall above
her head, or the bleached
white tablecloth spread

over the circle
that eats up so much
of the room's rectangle:

white not as a
tabula rasa
but as the infinite

color wheel, hinted at
in the violet
grays, pale yellows,

hollows and shadows
that serve to heighten
what nobody knows.

2.
My Dining Room, c. 1883–86

Nobody there—just the hasty, single
chair in the foreground. You can almost hear
the diner scraping it back so that
he can leap up and go on painting it,

yet not before tucking it in partway
again to make the white tablecloth
buckle and pull, that's good, a contrast
to the starchy drop (as in pinafores

he paints on little girls) of shadows
from another side of the table's square.
The great portraitist is alone today,
although the heaped whites near the whorl

of that dish look like napkins from a finished
meal, and the two wine bottles suggest . . .
Wait, more empty plates. The guests
may not have come; may be expected.

Good and bad news. He's a wit, he's social,
and sitters are his bread and butter.
Still—can we please not interrupt him
lest we spoil it all?

MARCEL PROUST: THREE POEMS

Anton Van Dyck

The sweet pride of hearts, the noble grace of things,
Shining in eyes, in velvets, in the trees;
The fine high language of address and dress,
The inborn vanity of women and kings!
Van Dyck, you're a triumph; you're the prince of calm
Gestures in these fine creatures soon to die,
In every trusting hand that beautifully
Still knows to open: look, she spreads her palm!

A halt under pines for the riders; nearby, a spring
Calm as they are, yet like them, close to sobbing:
Royal children, already grand and grave;
Defeated clothes, hats feathered to be brave,
And jewels like flooded flames, which somehow fill
These proud souls with the mounting bitterness
Of tears they refuse to let rise to their eyes.
And you in the pale-blue chemise, you above all,
Precious stroller, one hand propped on haunch,
In the other a leafed fruit plucked from a branch,
I can only dream of what's meant by your look
in this shady grove: upright but comfortable.
Duke of Richmond! Oh young sage! Or charming fool?
The banked fire of the sapphire at your neck
Is soft as your gaze . . . it keeps me coming back.

Chopin

Chopin, ocean of sobs and tears, of sighs
Above whose waves of sadness play a swarm
Of never-resting, dancing butterflies!
Dream, love, suffer, cry out, cradle, charm,
Always between attacks of pain you pour
An oblivion as dizzying and sweet
As the butterflies' caprice from flower to flower;
And so you find your grief and joy complicit:
The whirlwind thirsts for tears, and more, and more.
Soul mate of pale moon and sea, the prince
Of despair or noble lord betrayed, and all
The handsomer for your pallor, still you thrill
To the flood of sun into your sickroom, since
It weeps in smiling and in seeing suffers . . .
Smile of regret along with hopeful tears!

For Madeleine Lemaire

What subtle orchard-thief has skulked about
To snip these luminous grapes my lips love so?
A chance breeze blows these candles, makes them billow,
And is just soft enough not to snuff them out.

But no, for a paintbrush you set aside the yarn
And spindle, and bested God: made endless spring;
And it was to the lily and the climbing
Rose you went for your colors, Madeleine.

Your beauty may be frail, not to endure,
Yet like flowers of one day lives nonetheless
Immortally: all the carnations, lilies,
Or lilacs you painted, Madeleine Lemaire.

But you—who will paint *you,* fair gardener
Who every spring brings forth so many flowers?

TRIANGLE

Size and shape of a billiard rack,
but not so packed; a frame
of reference for radiance,

it once had crowned an altarpiece
in Santa Croce. Why is it here?
What does it matter? Eternity

travels, and would just as soon
shimmer on a museum wall
in San Diego for a while.

Three profiled angels on each side
of the Father make the Trinity
He tops top of your mind,

distracted, though, by those two holding—
what? Long-handled mirrors for
gazing at their own gorgeousness?

No, what Giotto's got to do
is make God in man's image and
render His resplendence as

intolerable, so that this pair
of angels must lift shields (I see
at last that's what these are) before

their eyes; meantime the other four,
bright-winged beauties all, get by
with a mere hand as visor.

Which raises then the question: why
don't they all turn away? And why
can't I stop myself from looking

at them looking-but-not-looking
at the thing that dazzles them,
not Godhead and not even paint

but the triangulating point
which is belief? Not quite: again.
This might be what I mean:

if, say, God's light could torment
even the willing angels, this
is how I believe they'd look.

THE GOLFERS

From a distance I can see the golfers (men
of a certain age and bulge, not fat or thin,
faces under receding hairlines pink
despite their visors) gathered on the green.
Pink and green are the chipper clothes that link
them in their silent circle as they lean
together toward the hole where one must sink
his white ball next.
                          Or that's what I can think
because, like them, I've lived now long enough
to put a scene in context; to guess at stories
of shifting rivalries, jokes turning rough
last week at the Clubhouse, and the joy
this Saturday for each one, still a boy,
of tracking gravity's trajectories.
But if I'd never seen a golf course, what
might I have thought?
                          I might have read that one
hole they were addressing as a grave,
a first goodbye within the congregation
of solemn brothers. And so, in fact, that huddle
seemed for an instant, until I shook it off.
Today? Today was fun and just the middle.

CRUISE

What does it mean, the ship shaped like an iron
skimming some unending bolt of sea
and rather than smoothing, wrinkling as it goes?
Right to left, guided by some right-handed
invisible god, it parts the waters slowly,
indifferent to what's troubled in its wake—
is that what I see, indifference? On the glossy,
backlit surface of the TV screen
the cruise commercial presses its own vision
of beauty, infinite sun filmed by a drone,
although to be one person means one porthole
and this is mine. One mind in which one image
of possible trillions plays repeatedly,
right to left, now headed to a future
that reads like the blue oceans of the past.
I'm standing here before clean loads of laundry,
the iron passing right to left, then lifted
time after time by my own wrinkling fist.

HAT DAY

Early 70s.
Beautiful day. On the dorm
lawn, some guy happy

to watch his hat fly
off his head every time he
leaps for the Frisbee

fears nevertheless
getting bored. "How about if
we all put on hats?"

he calls to the group.
"How about if I go get
my camera, and

you all search your rooms
and come back with whatever
headgear you round up,

and I'll take a shot
of everyone wearing them?"
"I don't have a hat,"

says one girl, knowing
where one hangs in her closet;
she looks bad in hats.

She can't be the sole
unfun person, however,
nor can the others

who in no time find
their hats too, and assemble
beneath the oak tree,

two rows. In the back
stand tall cowboys and rabbis,
one wide-brimmed female

like a lead singer.
It's as if they're all posing
for a new album

and she's the Mary
to the Peters, the Pauls, and
the kneelers like me,

short at best, shorter
at the base of the photo,
floppy bonnet tied

underneath my chin
like Bo Peep, but I warned them—
I look bad in hats.

It's me. I was there.
I recognize David, and
the other David,

there's Sue; I even
have a sense of who's missing.
Elliott, Hattie—

Hattie, my roommate!
With a name like that, she should
be in the picture.

It's almost too good,
too funny to think about.
I must write and thank

the guy who posted
the snapshot on Flickr for
old friends to click on . . .

Old friends, I'm sorry,
it's lovely to see you, but
can I be honest?

Surely it happened,
but the truth is I can't call
up Hat Day at all—

I've had to invent
the whole memory, half a
century later.

PART FOUR

ISLAND DIARIES

I do want to like this fellow. I've been waiting
years for another Englishman to chat with.
Claims he's a duke, born and bred in Milan,
yet his English sounds quite native, if old-fashioned.
Talks a great deal, though most of what he says
seems to be nonsense. Says he's a conjurer
or was. And yet it seems miraculous
that I should find his footprint in the sand!

*

I think it was right in the end, my sudden choice
not to board the ship to Naples. Little chance
I'd have survived the trip—and to what purpose?
I'd stood on principle, and had my moment
gathering the sundry characters of my life—
enough to breathe the air of renunciation
with a sort of joy. Strange then, this morning,
as I took my daily walk along the shore,
to hear a fellow running up behind me.
Excitable sort. Babbled about a shipwreck
long ago, though naturally I'd have noticed
or even caused it, had I been in the mood.
Still, I can think of no other explanation
for his being dressed no better than Caliban,
in a heap of animal skins and foot-long beard.
Worse, he seems to think he's king of the island.
That's how he pitched himself to some poor wretch
whose footprints he once stumbled on, like mine,

and made his servant. Dead now, I understand—
from overwork? I resolved to tell him nothing.
Occasionally I miss my Ariel,
I dream about Miranda, so I must
not be entirely shut of human feeling . . .
I suppose I'm not averse to some company.
I do want to like this Crusoe, but so much
of what he says is hopelessly banal.

*

He says he broke his staff and drowned his books.
If you owned a magic wand on this uncharted
island, would you be fool enough to destroy it?
He felt some envy, maybe, seeing my tools,
and had to make something up. Still, I'm sorry
if he really did have books. I would have liked
something to read besides the Holy Bible.
Pleased at first to hear his unlikely stories,
now I doze off. The man lives in the past,
harping on the crimes of his wicked brother
halfway around the world. He rose above it,
he says; points out he pardoned everyone
who'd ever wronged him, and let them go their way.
What does he want, applause? What I want to say is:
if you wish to be a Christian, do some chores.

*

How maddening to be lectured about labor.
What does he want from me—that I should sink
to asking him like a wife, "How was your day?"
Isn't it good enough he chops the wood
and pens the animals and sows the seeds

and knows he has; must he also narrate
his errands one by one? And if I understand
his story, his wrecked ship was packed with men
he was happy to see sold into enslavement.
How did I end up chums with this middlebrow?
The solitude he found me in was a blessing,
no burden, though it appear so to a man
who never had a thought that could be lost
or twisted by interruption. The villainy
I suffered in Milan, and on this island,
was nobler than his vacuous industry.
He made me see it: for that I'll give him thanks.

*

Given how impractical he is
I have to hope, for his sake, he dies first.
How would he manage old age all alone?
Prospero! The name ought to be mine;
I'm the one here who taught himself to prosper.
I'm proud of what I've done, but I'm not vain.
Vanity's his ultimate attribute
as he gazes like Narcissus in a pot
of clear water, and is charmed to find it wrinkling
with the image of his weathered face. Myself,
I look into the pot and know I made it;
see water neither of us can live without.

*

Apparently, he used up the India ink
he salvaged from a shipwreck. Think how much
loftier use I might have made of it . . .
As for this berry-essence he concocted,

it fades, I see now, even as I scribble.
And yet I remind myself I must cast off
not merely this diary, but recollection
itself. To the extent I live in time,
I dream now of the future: that my daughter
and her husband find their way to a safe harbor
and take joy in their progeny, as I've done . . .
Oh let her not have perished on the ocean
or in childbirth. Strange to be so ignorant
of what is happening! Or what may happen yet.

*

I think I have no choice but to forgive him.
Last night in his sleep he talked of elves
that run with "printless feet." The poor man wakes
startled as if from his own opened grave,
amazed to find that all his vivid dreams
have melted into thin air. Of course I wish
these banquets he describes were real enough
for me to eat; or that my salt-stained garments
could be refreshed in a twinkling, like the ones
he brightened with no dye, or so he says.
And reminds me I wasn't there. His velvet cloak,
which looks a little like the heavy curtain
that drops down to the stage at a play's conclusion,
is fraying and could use some of that magic.

*

We've settled into a sort of sexless marriage,
tolerant of the other's limitations;
sometimes, even, a little of our own.
I keep it to myself I can't call up

my own wife's countenance. I know I loved her;
but it seems to me, increasingly, as if nothing
not written in these lines has ever happened.
I can't explain it to a man like Crusoe.
Does he even think of women? If he ever
were lucky enough to take one, like a pet,
I hardly think he'd mention her with more
than a sentence in his tally of adventures.
Yes, I've seen him "writing." Well, so be it.
I never disclose my wish not to be rescued,
lest he should think me mad. I never tell this man
mired in dailyness and in false hope
that everything we record here will be bleached
white in the sun, or washed out with the tide.

*

The most astonishing thing. Last night I dreamed
I had a part in the life of Prospero.
The noble Neopolitan, Gonzalo,
smiled and invited me to tell my story,
and I gratefully complied. I met Miranda,
as shy as a Madonna as she held
a swaddled baby—was it boy or girl?—
and gazed up at Ferdinand, himself as fine
a specimen of manhood as I'd heard;
even the drunken butler was enchanting.
So many people! All of them looked at me—
Caliban, who stood straight to meet my eye,
Antonio, who was silent but not sullen—
with a level familiarity, as if
they'd always known I'd join their company.
I had made landfall on some sort of Heaven.
Then Ariel was flying, and so I flew

following him—or her—I can't be sure;
and although I never caught up, I could scan
from that height the whole island. And knew all
the years I'd thought myself alone, or nearly,
apart from the time with Friday, I had been
mistaken. Down there, gatherings of people
were making fires, as if to send out signals—
I couldn't tell. They might prove my enemies,
I thought. And yet why think so? As the smoke
began to obscure their movements, I woke up.

I looked to the bedding next to me: he was gone.
Prospero was gone! Well, he always
walks the beach in the morning; I knew where.
Low tide: good. Simple to track his footprints
along the sand, just as I had the first time.
And yet I saw no mark. I called his name,
racing back to our "castle," as I term it
(though he never was amused). Prospero!
Prospero! I called. It was then I spotted
the velvet cloak, his doublet, everything.
He has no other clothes; took none of mine.
But had I seen them? Now the clothes were gone.
No diary left either, nor his quill.
He had vanished—truly vanished, like my dream,
as if he and all he'd told me were a dream—
and left not a rack behind. (What is a rack?
That was his phrase: "leave not a rack behind.")

And yet if I were dreaming, how could I,
mere sailor, laborer, and thorough bore—
yes, that's how he thought of me, and was too vain
to note I knew it—have made up *his* own story?
Invented names like "Trinculo"? Concocted

a magician, as if I were one myself?
No, I refuse to believe it. He was here.
And though he tried so hard to disappear
from his own mind, my own is sharp and present.
I'll use it to invent some hardier ink
for copying all this out again. And leave it,
even if I've been sent back to my Maker,
for whoever may arrive upon these shores—
or already lives here. Someone will want to read
about our histories mashed up together,
Friday and Prospero, Ariel and me—
though it may lose some luster in my telling.

PART FIVE

FRUITCAKE

When Marianne Moore, thanking her friend
Elizabeth Bishop for a gift,
writes, "It is the one exciting
fruitcake in my experience,"

what do we make of this? Does Moore
wish to lampoon herself, or fruitcakes,
or both, or does she honestly
not guess she's funny? Chances are

she is well aware, and at fifty-five
is squarely in the business of
underscoring the caricature
of the eccentric she always was.

Are we predictably
singular too? If we bring joy
to others sometimes, will that do?
How long can we fend off the ennui

of our idiosyncrasies?
When Moore writes Dr. Williams, "Your poems
have a life, a style, that should not surprise me
but does; like dew-drops on the coat

of a raccoon," we may want to answer
"Raccoons are irrelevant here,
even as surprises, and furthermore
nobody thinks you saw those dew-drops,"

but her game anticipates us. We shake
the dew off our coats; resolve not to say
Miss Moore is nutty as a fruitcake,
because *that* is a cliché.

Never expected! Always fresh!
We must be; never, though, as nutty
as Mother, who chloroformed the cat
one day when Marianne was out

because her attachment was too great.
Poor, elated Robert Lowell
grew weary of both lunacy
and repeated bouts of getting well,

of stepping backward down his "ladder
to the moon." "I'd never drown myself,"
someone said he said. "But if I had
a button I'd switch myself off."

EGGS

William Bailey, 1974

1
A dozen of them:
removed from the carton, they
had to be counted.

2
That was the first thing.
To see I'd done that, myself
cupped in convention.

3
Eggs were beginnings.
No thoughts in their heads yet of
numbers or boxes.

4
No plan to be grouped
by some human in random
non-random groupings

5
so that I might say
"they're like balls come to rest in
a game of bocce";

6

no plan to roll off
or not roll off the table,
no, not a table

7

but this shallow shelf
in the middle of what is
not really nowhere

8

despite the flat paint
on the flat wall behind it,
almost the same plane;

9

almost the same brown,
but which differs, I think, to
about the degree

10

you might separate
the white of this egg from the
white of this other.

11
My two eyeballs stare.
At some point they start to
believe they can hear

12
the twelve tones up there,
whole notes of the possible
implied in the score.

JURY DUTY

In the great hall of the War Memorial Building
the jurors are waiting.

They're on folding chairs, and wearing their sticker-badges;
it's all so boring

sitting there till your number's up, not knowing
if you'll be serving

at all, and if so, for weeks on end or a day,
that in the beginning

some of them find themselves leaning back and squinting
to read the engravings

("Meuse-Argonne; 79th Division")
on the massive moldings

lining the thirty-foot ceiling, although by now
the words mean nothing.

*

Most people are checking their phones. Not many books.
One woman is chuckling

at a cat video in her palm, and one old fellow
who was neatly folding

and unfolding his actual, physical newspaper
gets up: he's walking

68

along the polished marble walls to study
the bronze plates listing

by county (for easy reference by family members,
not one still living)

all the dead doughboys of the state; he stops,
he reads, keeps going.

*

And now, forced television. A football movie
about guys grunting

and slamming helmet to helmet; then there's one,
if you aren't looking

when the opening credits run, or are hard of hearing,
which seems to be something

about the Nazis, until the special effects
confirm you're watching

Captain America, a futuristic soldier
from the past of cartooning.

Even the most resistant among the jurors
are caught consulting

the exploding screen now and then; after a while
they all are paying

so much attention, the clerk seems rude to call them:
he's interrupting.

*

It's time he escorted some jurors across the street
to another looming

old edifice, the colonnaded courthouse,
its white face baking

impartially in the sun. Fresh air! The jurors
can't help rejoicing.

A man sleeps on a bench. Past a boarded-up shop
some trash is blowing.

The jurors are still happy. They'll never complain
again, they're thinking,

if they can get off; on such a nice day, who would opt
to spoil it hearing

about people hurting each other, or to have to say
which ones are guilty?

LAST WORDS

Forgive me for not writing sober,
I mean sooner, but I almost don't
dare see what I write, I keep mating mistakes,
I mean making, and I'm wandering
if I've inherited what
my father's got.

I first understood it when he tried
to introduce me to somebunny:
"This is my doctor," he said,
then didn't say more, "my daughter."
The man kindly nodded
out the door.
I thought: is this dimension
what I'm headed for?
I mean dementia.

Not Autheimer's, but that kind he has,
possessive aphasia: oh that's good,
I meant to say progressive.
Talk about euthanasia!
I mean euphemasia,
nice words inside your head not there,
and it's not progress at all.

No, he's up against the boil
after years now of a sad, slow wall
and he's so hungry,
I mean angry.

Me too. I need to get my rhymes in
while I still mean. I mean can.

THE FIRE

In the living room, the night before the memorial,
they all pitched in to make a nice occasion
of building a fire. Some brought in snowed-on logs
to stack up by the hearth, while others came
too late with kindling, or proposed a better
way to layer firewood in the future.
Whatever was annoying was put up with,
the point being, in a family, that forbearance
could be itself a thing to keep you warm.
The bottom logs were blazing now and crumbled
loudly to ashen shapelessness, far gone
as the demented old man they remembered,
but no, nobody meant to think that horror—

not of his cremation which had happened
days ago, they all knew, though they were glad
not to know the hour precisely; they only saw
how the original logs had been essential
and yet dispensable, because that's right
or grows to be right; and there the metaphor
of fire breaking down broke down, because
wood will get poked and prodded, rearranged,
and who ever said life promised to be fair?
Some younger ones might go before, whose faces'
flawless glow the leaping flames highlighted,
and those who now were oldest knew it best
and hoped against hope, each one, to get there first.

HOT WATER BOTTLE

You're so long dead
and the days when you tended
your teenaged daughter go back so far
that the two of us seem
equally prehistoric.

But today for some
reason, or none—
which happens more and more often—
you resurfaced, like those
secret stabs in the gut
I'd have to endure at school.
I always forgot how bad it was
until another month had passed.
I always forgot I'd need you again
to soothe me, home from the wars at last,
with a cup of tea and the vaguely
vulva-like red rubber
hot water bottle.

You'd make sure the bottle's stopper
was dialed tight as an oven timer.
An electric heating pad
would have done the trick,
but you preferred to be on call
when the scalding bottle cooled;

to shuffle back to the kitchen, unplug
the thing and empty it in the sink
glug glug and start again.

You lived to see the birth
of my first daughter
but not the second.
That time my water broke all at once,
streamed down my legs,
flooded the front of my thin spring skirt
as I stood barefoot on the grass,
happy and afraid.

Somebody left on earth should know
that when I was young
you doted on me.
I'd lie on the couch,
hot water bottle on my flat
abdomen, and watch TV.
A rerun of *The Red Balloon*,
I'm thinking now.
One time I know it was that.
Whenever it was I saw it,
I remember the tug
of wishing I could catch the bobbing
string for the boy
as his red balloon drifted away.

FORGETTING NAMES

Inevitable, and not
too shaming that I forget
(long in years as I am)
some familiar name
for a moment or two;

but waking now it occurs
to me something worse
is already well on its way,
the perfectly normal day
that nobody anywhere,

no tip of any tongue,
will even think of trying
to call me up from the vast
data cache of the past:
the forgotten name is mine.

A LETTER TO LEENA

I came when you were born,
but soon the flying stopped.
By the time I came again,
we drove in private cars

and masked our public faces
like bandits bent on crimes
that had already happened;
once home, we'd wash our hands

of greed and disregard
while in the streets, more fists
were raised against long years
of violent injustice.

Born into an era
possibly too late
to salvage the green earth
a virus has made sure

you've barely seen so far;
born amidst decline
of all sorts—when the rule
of idiocy emerged

finally as malice,
and patience, that slim virtue
of the citizen, exposed
the privilege of guilt—

you, oh wide-eyed girl,
have joined that ancient global
club of generations
whose first days seem our last.

Civilizations do
end, and there's no reason
we shouldn't be the ones
to close out the whole series;

we're halfway out the door now,
a techno-human species.
Is it too much to hope, though,
you'll get a whole life in?

I'm thinking more in days
at the moment. How many days
do I get to spend with you
before we must pack up

and drive with some unclear
motive back to the spot
we are supposed to stay?
Why leave you, anyway?

Nothing sweeter than waking
and waiting for you to wake.
Breast milk in your belly,
you wriggle and coo and kick

and smile and smile at us
as if we were the prime
source of infectious joy—
but that's you, of course.

Remember, I keep saying
inside my head, because
I have words. *Remember this:*
Leena at three months.

I got to give you a bottle.
I got to fondle your feet.
And it's all a replay from
the lost days I recall

when your mother was this new.
I got to have it twice,
her and her sister. Then
a third time: I got you.

How could such floods of love
not add up to enough?
Yet I hardly tried at all
to make this old world better;

what I made was dinner
and poems, when I could.
Dear child in a bassinet,
who tries and tries and can't

quite roll over yet,
grow to turn your mind
to the desperate demands
of your time; choose to be glad

to change, not to wait and see.
I'm changed by you already.
I want to be around
more keenly than before,

to live because you're living.
When you have words, I'll listen:
tell me what I'm missing
when you come to visit me.

Acknowledgments

Thanks to the editors of the journals, websites, and anthologies where the following poems first appeared, sometimes in slightly different form:

"The Fortune Cookie," "Fruitcake," "Last Words," and "Zoom Rooms" in *The American Scholar*

"Hat Day" and "Oak Hill, West Virginia" in *blog.bestamerican poetry.com*

"Jury Duty" and "Man-Barbies" in *The Hopkins Review*

"A Letter to Leena" in *The Common*

"The Fire" and "Mule Team and Poster" in *Literary Imagination*

"Carlo Crivelli and the Trees" and "Marcel Proust: Three Poems" in *Literary Matters*

"John Singer Sargent: Two Interiors" (excerpted as "John Singer Sargent: 'My Dining Room'") in *The Map of Every Lilac Leaf: Poets Respond to the Smith College Museum of Art* (Smith College)

"Forgetting Names" and "Orecchiette" in *Plume*

"Hot Water Bottle" in *Poems of Healing* (Everyman's Library)

"Italian Haiku" (excerpted as "Roman Haiku") in *Quarterly West*

"Vanitas" in *The Eloquent Poem: 128 Contemporary Poems and Their Making* (Persea Books)

"White Petals, 3 A.M." in *The Sewanee Review*

"St. Sebastian Interceding for the Plague-Stricken" in *Together in a Sudden Strangeness: America's Poets Respond to the Pandemic* (Knopf)

A NOTE ABOUT THE AUTHOR

Mary Jo Salter is Krieger-Eisenhower Professor in The Writing Seminars at Johns Hopkins University. She is the author of eight previous poetry collections and of a children's book, and is a coeditor of *The Norton Anthology of Poetry*. She lives in Baltimore.

A NOTE ON THE TYPE

This book was set in Scala, a typeface designed by the Dutch designer Martin Majoor (b. 1960) in 1988 and released by the FontFont foundry in 1990. While designed as a fully modern family of fonts containing both a serif and a sans serif alphabet, Scala retains many refinements normally associated with traditional fonts.

Composed by North Market Street Graphics,
Lancaster, Pennsylvania

Printed and bound by Friesens,
Altona, Manitoba

Designed by Soonyoung Kwon